LIFE: The Complete Handbook

LIFE

The Complete Handbook

This little book contains all you need to know
about LIFE and LIVING

by Stuart Rose

First published in 2024 by Arena Books

www.arenabooks.co.uk

Stuart Rose
LIFE: The Complete Handbook

A CIP catalogue record for this book is available from the British Library.

Thema: QDXB

ISBN: 978-1-914390-21-0 (paperback)
ISBN: 978-1-914390-22-7 (ebook)

Cover design by Anna Soevik

To Shaun, Maggie, and Sally

Other Writings by the Author:

108 Meditations on Silence, 2006
ISBN 9-84685-168-8
Sublime Love, 2007
Indica Books ISBN 818-6569 685*
Transforming the World, 2009
Peter Lang ISBN 3-03910-316-4
Who Are You? Really! 2010
O-Books ISBN 978-1-84694-343-0

Edited by the Author:
Energy & Space, 2009
The Dual Publishers ISBN 978-0-9562112-0-0
Highly Significant, 2010 (Web Published)
Tools of Understanding, 2011 (Web Published)
The Book of OM, 2022
Kaivalydhama S.M.Y.M.S. ISBN 978-81-952992-1-8*
*Only available through publishers' websites

In Progress:
Pictures / Collected Poems
Happily Disabled (2nd edition)

Contents

Introduction   1

Chapter 1: Existence is Everywhere   7

Chapter 2: The Universe and Cosmos   17

Chapter 3: Multiples of Every Thing   23

Chapter 4: Does God Exist?   31

Chapter 5: Knowing Love   55

Chapter 6: Fragility and Uncertainty   69

Chapter 7: Differences Between People   73

Chapter 8: Bodies   81

Chapter 9: Right or Wrong   97

Afterword 1: Answering what Life and Living is all About   109

Afterword 2: Truths: A Brief Summary   123

Epilogue   127

Introduction

This little book, LIFE, seeks to answer questions about life itself and the purpose of our existence by revealing the nine truths of life. It will mention "God" and questions linked to the idea of God like "Where do I come from?" and "Why do I exist?" many times. This is because the idea of God pops up in so many separate areas of interest when we are thinking about life. However, LIFE is not a book about religion or spirituality; it is a book that concentrates on life itself.

The nine truths of life serve as a timely reminder of who we really are. They encompass the most important aspects of our lives; everyone knows at least a little about all of them. Each chapter explores one of these truths, and readers will find that certain themes will be more important to them than others.

This book touches upon our human lives from before an individual exists, right through to after they have passed away.

The sources for the knowledge in this book have been taken from a wide variety of ancient and modern sources, and are brought together here in this concise pocket handbook. There are few references given; this is because the facts are already widely known and such references would be multiple and interfere with the book's flow.

The nine Truths of life are explored in the following chapters:

1. Existence Is Everywhere

Existence is the one constant in life. Every thing else changes. This chapter asks the question, "Is God existence?"

2. Universe and Cosmos

This chapter explores the difference between the Universe and the Cosmos. It looks at the possibility of more universes and asks whether God could physically be synonymous with space.

3. Multiples of Every Thing

Every thing in life is made up of multiples except one thing which is identified.

4. Does God Exist?

This chapter is divided into five parts in order to answer the question "Does God Exist?" It draws upon questions of geography and looks at statistical data in order to explore the question of why there are numerous religious beliefs when it is assumed that there is only one God. The questions is answered.

5. Knowing Love and the Purpose of Life

The purpose of love, life, and personal experience is examined in this chapter. The purpose and meaning of life are explored. Then we look at the difference between what we know as "love" and all other feelings, and the importance of the role of sex in love. The possibility of God's input into the phenomenon of love is explored as well as the role that human instinct plays.

6. Fragility and Uncertainty

From the moment of conception through to death, life is always under threat, but there is a possibility of acceptance and a survival instinct that compensates for this.

7. Differences

Equalities and inequalities will always exist unless we learn to look at life in a different way.

8. Bodies

This chapter paints a graphic picture of life and its stages. It then looks at how much has changed in the last 100 years and questions how the body will survive into the future.

9. Right or Wrong?

And lastly, the ninth part of life looks at the idea of right and wrong. It looks at how human beings make choices and demonstrates that each person already has the answers they might be so desperately looking for.

LIFE raises new questions about these truths and gives answers that are based on provable facts, as well as observations and experiences. There is space for readers to add notes and thoughts about each subject at the end of each chapter.

In many instances there are satisfactory answers, but in others, things are "known" without being provable. Some of these truths will be more familiar to readers than others. In reality, all the topics in the following chapters interweave in our lives, and it is in these combinations that truths about being human are revealed. We will start with the idea of existence itself.

Chapter 1

Existence is
Everywhere

The question of who we are aims at the very centre of our being, at our existence – both our collective existence, "we are", and our individual existence, "I am."

Perhaps it seems like a silly question to ask whether you or someone else exists – of course you do! Everyone, and everything that is reflected in the senses, exists. But where does this capacity to be, to exist, come from? Each person has it from the moment of their conception. Every living as well as every inert "thing" has it.

If this statement is true, then it begs the following

questions: How did each life come into being? What is each life for? And what is the meaning of it all?

We will see in the chapter "Bodies" that it is possible to answer questions such as what is the physical purpose of life, but the "how" and the "why" questions are not possible to answer definitively. However, we can come close, for example by exploring particular beliefs and faiths, or myths, traditions, or religions. We will look at this possibility in the chapter "Does God Exist."

The idea of "existence" is used so much by everyone – and it usually occurs without really thinking about its all-encompassing complexity. For example in speech, and indeed in thought, the pronoun "I" is used unconsciously or as shorthand to confirm the fact of a person's existence. People say, "I exist," or more commonly, "I am," as in, "I am going to the shops," "I am going to bed," "I am going for a walk."

Existence

Existence "exists." This is a proven fact which is known to be true by everyone through observation and through our senses. It is fact that a person cannot experience a state of non-existence. Even in deep sleep, and also when a person is fully unconscious, the person has to exist to be in that state.

There is no outside of existence that can be known or perhaps even imagined, which means that outside of existence does not exist. Ask yourself this question, "Can I possibly experience something outside of existence?" This is not a trick question. The answer is that it isn't possible.

No "thing"

It is certain that nothing exists without existence, so both something and everything, including nothing, need existence in order to exist. However, as nothing does not contain any "thing," as the word implies, it can only exist as a concept.

Types

As human beings, we do not currently know about more than one type of existence – although we can imagine alternative existences. We do so particularly in science fiction. But people don't experience gaps in their existence – it doesn't stop and start. Even in death it is a seemingly endless flow.

Imagine what life would be like if there were two different types of existence occurring at the same time. Life would be utter chaos. Thankfully, in our one life, we only have to "deal" with one existence. Even when a person loses consciousness, existence still exists for that person to "regain" it. Existence is totally complete. Nothing can be added-to, or taken away from, this one existence.

First "thing"

Existence is the name for the original "thing," the very first thing. I call it a "thing" here because there is no other word to use. There is nothing anywhere like it. This same "thing" is sometimes, perhaps incorrectly, called the "prime mover," "absolute reality," or "God" – depending on which scenario we are in.

Something other than existence could not have brought existence into existence because that something would need to have existed first. This has been shown to be impossible which means that existence has to be single and eternal; that is, without beginning or end. In religious scriptures, these are some of the words used to describe God. This may make people ask whether "God" and "existence" are the same thing.

No change

The existence that is experienced by us today seems not to have changed. There are no historical records of existence having changed at any time in the past despite everything else having changed. We can therefore safely say that it is not likely to change in the future. Existence is the only constant that there is anywhere in the whole Universe and beyond. Without exception, everything else moves and changes.

Existence is the only solid part of life that can be relied upon not to change. Bringing this fact right down to the level of the individual person, it means the statement "I am" is the only concrete (unchanging) thing that we can say about ourselves. This is true whether a person is young or old and regardless of their situation – happy or sad, sick or well, and so forth.

Everyone has the potential to realise this – a child can realise it, and a person near the end of their life can realise it in the same way; the "thing" that is existence will not have changed.

Bringing 'it' about

Existence cannot bring itself into existence because it would need to be in existence in the first place in order to do it. If it could, existence would thereby itself be impermanent and subject to change, which experience shows it isn't. We might say that anything that "moves" is, in this case, incomplete because it cannot be considered to be permanent and unchanging.

If something moves, it means that it starts, continues and stops, for instance, like rolling a ball. If existence could move it would leave space for an absolutely complete existence to exist that doesn't move which, as far as is known, hasn't happened and is unlikely to do so.

Single quality

Existence is experienced as a constant, and as a single, unchanging quality. We could say that existence is the original quality out of which all other qualities, such as natural order and multiples of nature, come. Existence is singular, not dual or multiple; as we have said, there can't be two different existences. If there were two, then the second would need to be different from the first; it would have different qualities. It would not be existence. How and why other qualities to the existence that is known might come about is not known.

Nothing unnecessary

Qualities other than existence have come about because, to the limits of our senses, they can be experienced in everything a person tastes, smells, sees, hears and touches. I have used the word "limits" here because we know that different creatures have different abilities regarding the sense – for example the extraordinary hearing of dolphins or the exception sight of birds. It can therefore be said that our senses are limited to the extent that is needed to experience them, which is the same for all life forms. Put another way, there seems to be nothing unnecessary or missing in the make-up and contents of our existence, of being a human. We can do all we can and nothing more.

Non-spatial

Existence is also non-spatial, which means that there is no particular place or places where existence exists. It exists everywhere there are things in order that they can exist, but it also exists beyond the material restrictions of shape, form and size. This could mean that, for example, existence is the same within a seemingly empty box as it is beyond the Universe.

Timeless

Experience shows that the same is true of the non-temporality of existence; existence is timeless. Time only begins with movement and, as has been shown, existence doesn't move, so it cannot be measured.

Indescribable

It is likely that pure, unalloyed existence is not aware of its own existence. It simply "is". If there is no second existence, then it is incomparable with anything else because there exists nothing like it. Existence cannot be described, it can only be accepted.

Existence doesn't do anything. It doesn't act. It can perhaps be thought of as the "stage" on which everything else appears to act; it doesn't change but the "scenery" appears to; it doesn't move but everything else appears to. Existence just Is.

What's the use of knowing more about existence?

Nothing can be done about it other than to accept what existence is and then move on with life. If a person believes that God is existence, then the situation can change for that person because knowing this could help to "enlighten" that person's religious belief.

Existence cannot be stopped even with death. It cannot be manipulated in any way. Existence just continues unendingly. People will come and go as will all life; the infrastructure of mountains, planets and galaxies will go too. All will continue until such time when every "thing" has gone, but existence will still remain, unchanged, just as it was before any thing existed.

Chapter 1 Truths:

- Without existence there can be no life.
- Existence is unlimited, everything else, such as all people, are limited.
- God cannot come before or after existence. Therefore God, if God exists, is synonymous with existence.

Jot down any thoughts you may have about "Existence is Everywhere":

Chapter 2

The Universe and Cosmos

The stars and sometimes planets can be seen in the night sky just by looking up. And through our evolving astronomic science and increasingly powerful telescopes, our knowledge of the Universe is building all the time. There are now space stations, excursions into space and "modules" venturing ever further into the great unknown. One theory about how the Universe came into being, into existence, is the "Big Bang theory."

Every "thing" in this Universe exists, of this we can be sure. All the "bits" of rock – whether tiny or gigantic – that are flying about in a seemingly aimless fashion in space, exist. And the component parts of the Big Bang, or whatever else caused the Universe to come into being, had to exist before this Universe could happen. Therefore, it is certain that there was existence before this Universe.

Cosmos

Interest in space is along two different yet overlapping pathways. One group sticks to provable facts about the Universe mostly in astronomy and physics, while Cosmologists have a wider view, on what can and cannot be proved by adding in philosophy, maths, and religious and other forms of knowledge.

The place in which this Universe exists – for it has to exist somewhere – was named the "Cosmos" by the ancient Greeks. To paraphrase William Shakespeare again, "All the Cosmos is the stage and everything on it merely players."

Very little is known about the Cosmos. It may be either be full of gases and various objects (because these things also exist in this Universe) or it might contain nothing at all. The Universe exists within the Cosmos, this seems to be known, but the extent of the Cosmos is not known. This means that the Cosmos could be the "stage" where other universes, if there are other universes, also exist.

There are two ideas about the extent of the Cosmos. On the one hand, the Cosmos cannot be infinite as it would need to be in existence first, that is, it would need to have been in existence before it existed, which sounds like nonsense! But in this line of thinking, like every "thing" in existence, the Cosmos would have to have started from something, continue, and then eventually cease to be.

The alternative idea is that the Cosmos is in fact infinite and has always been in existence. In this theory the Cosmos and existence must be synonymous - one and the same.

This space, the Cosmos, might therefore be seen as God, because God is thought to be everywhere, just like existence.

Contents of the Cosmos

The Universe is full of "stuff" such as stars, galaxies, planets, and gases. As far as is known, there appears to be no clear line or distinction between the Cosmos and the Universe. There seems to be some confusion between these two "objects". Up in the night sky, we say we see the Universe. But what we actually see are pinpricks of reflective light from solid entities (stars). The space in-between the stars, the dark night sky, is in fact the Cosmos which is comprised of gases and other "things" that are as of yet not fully known.

The Cosmos envelopes everything. That much is widely known. Therefore, it can be said that the Cosmos "holds" the Universe together. It physically surrounds every thing and that includes Planet Earth. The Cosmos holds the Earth's slender atmosphere. And who's to say that the Cosmos doesn't also infiltrate and run through everything – including everything on and in the planet we inhabit. This means that every thing, and every person, is in some way connected to everything else and also with that which extends to the very distant depths of space – with infinity.

Chapter 2 Truths:

- There was existence before this Universe.
- Every thing is connected to everything, everywhere.

Jot down any thoughts you may have about "The Universe and Cosmos":

Chapter 3

Multiples of

Every Thing

The Universe is packed full of multiple things rather than single, solitary items. For example, even a single cell cannot exist without the support of numerous other things in its environment. The only "thing" that is single and unrelated to anything else, is existence. There are no multiple existences because only one existence exists throughout everything. But, as existence cannot be fully known, what it *is* can only be accepted as it is experienced.

In one human body there are billions of things, as scientists tell us, all relating to each other, and all dependent upon each other. Existence has to be one hundred per cent perfect for every thing to work together – even though it might sometimes feel less than perfect for reasons beyond our understanding.

Chaos

The stability and pervasiveness of existence means that it can be seen not as a chaotic jumble of things but as a natural order with every thing in its place – all the countless number of things having their place and supporting each other. Nothing in excess, nothing missing. There is an uncountable number of things in just one human body, and there are billions of us.

At the conception of each person, many multiple things had to come together to cause the creation of that new thing – that person. For instance, for each new person to come into being, two main things are first needed – a mother and a father. The chance that these two people came together at this particular time and place is astonishing! After a new person comes into existence, a unique individual has been created that contains billions of multiple multiples. These billions of things aren't necessarily unique, but the totality, the final outcome, *is*. This is the story of all people, but also of every living thing – families, species, nations, and worlds.

How many

It is not known whether the Universe is on its own or is one of many universes, but bearing in mind that everything known, without exception, comes about in multiples which relate to other things, it is pretty safe to agree that there could be many universes. But where is the beginning of these possible multiples? How did the first Universe come about? How did it then multiply? Will it ever be known?

We can see no clear end to this process, to this seemingly endless universal motion, or energetic movement, of multiplying. It is easy to think of ourselves as individuals, not related to anything else, but nothing could be further from the truth. Every thing exists as bundles of multiple things all working together. All in a natural order.

Non-physical

So far, we have mentioned physical, material things, but the same is true for non-physical and subtle things too – things such as thoughts, emotions, communication through voice, electricity, wind, and even extra-sensory perception. Everything is always in motion; all are the sum of their parts, both physical and mental. When and how will this motion stop?

All things stop eventually but according to scientists, the event in which all things as we know them stop, at the same time, could be a very long way away in time. We know that all individual things stop at some point – this can be seen everywhere. It is the nature of things. The date of a natural ending, the death of a particular thing, cannot be known in advance but, regardless, ending will come to every body and every thought, every thing and everywhere. Medical and other sciences can intervene and delay the natural order for a living being, but the end will come nonetheless.

Purpose

There is much talk and questioning about the purpose of existence and, even more so, of the purpose of our individual lives. Purpose with regard to the former is completely unknown other than existence can be said to hold everything in place. Whereas in the answer to the purpose of our individual lives, we know that all life has similar characteristics; it starts, it continues, it generally multiplies and then it ends.

Inanimate objects, like mountains and galaxies, came into being, are sustained, and then disintegrate. This is the natural order. There appears to be no other order than this. Even an unnatural life (if there were to be such a thing) starts, is sustained, and ends.

One might say therefore, that life's basic and primary purpose is to exist (stay alive) and multiply, nothing more and nothing less. What happens during a living being's existence is that it grows, sustains (as well as fruits or multiplies), and decays. Plus (at least for a person), there can be a mixture of sensual experiences, such as happiness and sadness, highs and lows, and everything else in between birth and death.

Perhaps only human beings have the capacity to ask about life's purpose. Yet, if the answer to life's purpose is clear, perhaps what we really mean when we ask this is, "What is the *meaning* of my life?" This is the more important question.

Meaning

Throughout history, no single idea about the over-arching meaning of life has been adopted universally. Various religions and traditions provide multiple, mostly similar, codes of practice and ideal life outcomes. In many cultures in the twenty-first century, a person can choose which of these ideas is most true for them. For many people, the idea that life continues in some shape or form after death is an attractive idea. Usually, this idea involves the belief that an individual's life has some meaning beyond what we know as being alive – and that there exists some kind of redemption or resurrection after death.

Today, meaning is left up to each person to establish and develop, or not, as they wish; each person lives by their individual choice. They might choose to accept that life has no meaning at all, and that the objective of life is to simply lead a happy and contented life.

Others choose to believe that the continuation of some form of life is dependent on performance in this life.

Some believe that the body is discarded while life itself continues in various alternative realms – either continuing ad infinitum, or reaching a real conclusion at some future time.

But there are always multiple choices, multiple

mysteries (about God and other things). These will be further explored in the next chapter.

Chapter 3 Truths

- The only single "thing" that exists is existence itself. All other things are multiple.
- Life's purpose is to exist and multiply.
- There is no given, universal meaning to life.

Jot down any thoughts you may have about "Multiples of Everything":

Chapter 4

Does God Exist?

This chapter is made up of four sections: firstly, an introduction to the question; secondly, an exploration of personal (individual) beliefs; thirdly, a broad look at social beliefs; and finally, an answer to the question, "Does God exist?"

Section 1: An Introduction to the Question

Throughout human history, most people have had thoughts about who they are and where they stand in the world. Many conclude that there has to be something better, or *more*, than the life that we perceive around us every day. But what that something *is* (of which there are many variations) has always been a mystery.

In this chapter, the main focus is to answer the question about God's existence. Before we begin, and for clarification, it should be noted for many people of various religions, much emphasis is placed on an in-between figure, rather than God.

These figures are well known, for example, Jesus in Christianity, Krishna in Hinduism, and Mohammad in Islam. These in-between figures are real, historical, people – people who can be physically visualised and learned about. As real people (whether historical or imagined) they can be more readily engaged with than the unknowable and abstract concept of God.

This concept of the relatable human being who stands between people and God, is a focus of all theistic religions. However, the subject of this chapter is not about these figures, but rather about the existence of God.

What comes first

The religious teachings cause a major problem. In the first chapter of this book, we concluded that no existence was possible before existence! If God existed before existence, then God would have had to bring existence about. If existence was created, then this would mean that existence is not eternal. If it was brought about by something else (like God), then consequently it would have a beginning, a middle, and an end. Moreover, God would have needed to be in existence in order to exist.

Similarly, if God came after existence, it would allow the possibility of there being more than one God.

The answer, seems to therefore be, that God (if God does indeed exist) and existence, are one and the same.

This concept is not new. Perhaps one of the earliest examples comes from the very ancient Indian thinkers. These individuals told of the start of duality, that is, the start of life. Their thinking was that a single outpouring from the One then divided into two – conceived of for example, as Spirit, Soul or male on the one hand, and Primal Order or female on the other hand.

In these belief systems, it was thought that everything came into being out of this duality. In Sanskrit, the word for male is *Purusha* and the word for female is *Prakriti* – they are the unmoving and the moving. These two branches – Purusha and Prakriti – came from Brahman, the gender-neutral Sanskrit name for the very beginning of everything. This tripartite concept has similarities to the trinity which is found in later religions.

These religious scriptures were passed down orally through the generations, and written, a very long time ago, but also obviously a very long time after the beginning of the world. They did not have the scientific knowledge that we have today. These writings were instead based on a mixture of (some) facts, untruths, hearsay, and myth. Yet, even if we add the huge advances that have been made in astronomy and scientific knowledge – knowledge that has possibly reached the far edges of the Universe – people are still none the wiser about the existence of God. The mystery still remains.

Section 2: An exploration of personal (individual) beliefs

One of the consequences of not asking this question, of not asking whether God exists or not, is the (seemingly cold) possibility that human life is meaningless. We are then left with the possibility that a person lives, like most animals, until they are eaten by a faster or stronger animal, or until they die of disease, starvation, or old age.

This is not a comfortable thought for most people, hence the attraction to mystery, and to the possibility of God. But only one of these options can be true – either the mystery or the cold "reality." The lack of factual evidence means that we have never been able to verify the truth and the question therefore continues to vex many people's minds.

But this a simplified picture of how a person lives. Life doesn't necessarily include adherence to a particular religion. Many people do belong to one religion or another, either strongly or less so, through their choice or through social reasons which are discussed below and in the next section. Also, many people don't follow a particular religion in any involved way but they still believe in the presence of God in varying shapes and forms.

Additionally, there are people, a minority globally, who think that what we see is all there is. They believe that the only things in existence are those things that can be sensed. They believe that there is no mystery, and no God. One example of a belief system that falls under this category is humanism; humanists accept everything that can be seen, nothing more. They argue that, life is OK as it is – that life can be beautiful and fulfilling, all the more so if it is worked hard for.

For others who don't believe in anything other than what can be perceived, life can seem meaningless and empty. For these people, it can sometimes seem that bleakness, chaos, and anarchy are taking over the world – and indeed for them, they frequently are.

Alternatively, what would life be like if it was known for a fact that the mystery surrounding the existence of God was all found to be true? What if it were proved that God exists? What if God could be seen, heard, and touched?

But do people want a God who can be really and factually known? If this were to occur, the mystery of God would be lost. Everything surrounding the image built over thousands of years, all the characteristics that have been developed, all ideas of an idealised "promised land" would all be gone.

Or would they? Most religions tell us that God gives every individual the ability to choose whether to believe in God or not. But do we choose to believe that God created existence? Or do we believe that God is the product of humankind's collective imagination? Or the product of socialisation? Or just of wishful thinking?

The majority of people who are religious, and who believe that God exists, are likely happy with their idea of God; there appear to be few calls for God to change. It seems to be accepted by people who believe in God, that God doesn't answer all prayers. Believers also accept the idea that God allows things like illness, starvation, and wars to occur. Everyone also has to accept that individual life as a human being on Earth has to end.

Numbers

A survey of the world population carried out in 2020 by Pew Research Centre found that a vast proportion, perhaps over 80% or more of the world's population, "identify with a religious group." This study was undertaken via the analysis of over 2,500 censuses from a total of 230 countries and territories worldwide. The main religions recorded were Christianity 32%, Islam 23%, Hinduism 15%, and Buddhism 7%. About 16%

of people described themselves as not affiliated with any religion.

This research does not necessarily prove that all those people affiliated with different religions actually believe in God. But it does indicate that there are many, many people who at least hope that God, or a "supreme Being", or just something higher than themselves that they cannot describe, does exist.

As we have said, belief in God cannot be approached with known facts because there aren't any. Belief can only come through a study of various (religious or otherwise) teachings, and then by expanding this knowledge through the intellect, and through faith, prayer, hope and imagination.

Qualities

Before we further tackle our original question about the existence of God, we need to explore the qualities that we expect to find in God.

The principal characteristics of God, as God is described in the scriptures of all the major religions (Christianity, Hinduism, Islam and others) are: omnipotence (that God is all-powerful), omniscience (that God is all-knowing) and omnipresence (that God is everywhere). Anything less, and we are not talking about God.

Looking at these terms in more detail reveals just how difficult they are to accept. For instance, if God is all-powerful, then it would imply that no-one other than God has any power. It means that the power which a person might think is theirs and can see the results of around them, is not theirs at all but wholly God's. The word "omnipotent" therefore means that believers exist solely as instruments for God and that anything thought to be carried out by them as individuals is a misconception.

Taking this idea further, if God is all-powerful, then many people would find it difficult to accept that God allows individuals to carry out acts that are negative or damaging to other people. And moreover, if these acts are carried out by people, then how can it be said that God has all the power? And if God is anything less than all-powerful, then what we think of as God is not God. Anything less than all-powerfulness would allow another god to be superior – and this is not an idea that is believed in any of the major religions.

To continue. How does a person do what she or he thinks they do? For example, how does a person raise their hand in the air? Yes, there is a physiological answer, but this is incomplete! The reality is that people just don't know the full picture of how their actions and thoughts occur. And, because every question of this kind is unanswerable in full, it is likely that, consciously or unconsciously, incomplete answers are accepted as the whole truth. What else can a person do?

This also applies to the other characteristics of God. If God is omniscient, all-knowing, then it means that God is present in each and every thought, and even provides the ability to have thoughts. Did the brain function and evolve all on its own? In all creatures? Or did something omniscient bring these things into being, and continue to make these things function?

Similarly, if God is not omnipresent (everywhere) then, as mentioned, it would enable the possibility that a greater God – who *is* omnipresent – exists. "Everywhere" means inside, around, and throughout each person, all creatures, and every thing – every thing that exists in the Universe. There can be no gaps, no exceptions!

Every "thing," every "how," and every "where." These three characteristics of God are extremely difficult to accept as fact – and this is one of the reasons why people have beliefs; although things can't be proven, everyone has beliefs in order to make sense of the world and to create some degree of certainty in an uncertain world.

Present but Separate

As well as these characteristics, God has another characteristic. It is believed by billions of people that God, in some indescribable form, is both immanent (directly personal) as well as transcendent (totally other). Most people who describe themselves as religious or spiritual believe that God can help them is some way – that God "listens" to them, creates circumstances for them. They believe that God can help them through their trials and tribulations, can help them with their life as a spiritual force or guide.

This is not dependent on whether a specific religion is followed or not. God is thought by many to be an entity, a "someone" who can be communicated with through contemplation, prayer, or just being silent – and who can answer in some inexplicable way. This is not to say that people believe that God

41

necessarily has any human characteristics, far from it. The conundrum is that God is believed to have the ability to be closely present, even within, a person, while at the same time being far away and far outside – both immanent and transcendent.

Continuing with numbers

In religion, it is these three characteristics that define what is meant by the term "God". But what of the sizeable minority of around 16% of people who class themselves as unaffiliated? These people do not "know" a personal God – at least not so clearly or specifically as those who are active participants in any of the various religions – but they still believe, however vaguely, in a "Higher Power." Many people in this unaffiliated category believe in something else – in an "energy" or just something else or something more.

Many of these people believe that there is some thing far greater than themselves that is in ultimate control and that their life continues after death somehow.

So this division of people's religious or spiritual beliefs – this breaking down into percentages and statistics – is artificial; there are many grey areas, and people do not necessarily fit neatly into one category or another. For many people, their beliefs in the 20th Century draw from every religious idea, and from any source, in the world.

Finally, we remember the small minority of people, particularly but not exclusively comprised of Humanists, who believe that there is nothing greater than what we see in this world. They believe in nothing greater than themselves. These people draw strength from a whole range of influences and each other in their attempt to live life to the full without the influence of any form of personal God.

Section 3: A Social God

Geography

Now we take our attention away from the individual and to social groups. There are many religious and social ideas that exist in the world (usually the social ideas come out of the religious ideas and are indistinguishable). Are any of them right?

Historically and still in the twenty-first century, religions are geographically located. There is Christianity spreading originally from the Mediterranean region mostly west to Europe and the Americas; Hinduism staying mostly in India; Islam from the Middle East spreading mostly east but also today (as with Christianity) existing in pockets everywhere.

Then there is Buddhism that exists mainly in Asia. China has a mix of Buddhism and Socialism. Sikhism exists mostly in north west India, and Zoroastrianism (including Parsees) in Iran and India. Religions and religious ideas cover the whole world and exist in every culture. But no one religion has been adopted fully everywhere and by all peoples.

Religious groups have often disagreed with each other, and have often struggled and fought internally. For example, Protestant and Catholic Christians in Northern Ireland; Orthodox Christian Russians fighting fellow Orthodox believers in Ukraine; Sunni and Shia Muslims in some Middle Eastern countries; Christians and Muslims in former Yugoslavia and in the Middle East, especially Syria; Buddhists against Muslims in Burma (Myanmar); communist China against Muslims at one place and Buddhists at another, and more.

This happens despite the fact that most of these

religions believe that there is only one God. The historical disagreements, rivalries and even wars – that have often occurred over decades or centuries – often turn into incomprehensible muddles that can be bloody.

Economics

What does this mean? And why, if there is only one God, isn't there just one religion? The answer to these and many other similar questions, is humankind. Throughout history and in many regions, why have the strong forced their religions onto the weaker, or the less technologically, or militarily, advanced societies? On the other hand, in recent times in particular, why have many people migrated taking their religion and culture with them? The answer to both questions is nothing to do with God but is related to economics or to persecution – in other words, for worldly reasons – as will be shown.

Section 4: Conclusion

Now we can get closer to an answer to our original question – Does God exist? The answer brings us into two directions which are not either/or but the latter may be held by the majority of the former

- in fact this result would be surprising if it were not so. This might sound confusing so here is the explanation.

Previously, the answer to "Does God exist?" in the main depended on an individual's birthplace and the family into which he or she was born. A child would normally follow the parents because that particular religion was the core of that society – a society's religion would be the glue that held people together.

If a person was born in the United Kingdom before the time of King Henry VIII, Roman Catholicism would have been the standard household religion. After the time of King Henry VIII it was Protestantism. If one was born in France around this time, the norm would have been Roman Catholicism; if Russia, then Orthodox Christian; if Iran, then Shia Islam; if Pakistan, then Sunni Islam; if Thailand then Theravada Buddhism; if Japan then Mahayana Buddhism and Shinto, and so the list goes on.

The religion that ends up being followed by an individual mainly depends on where that child's birth took place, and the society and the religion followed by that society. So geographical location has a huge effect on a person's particular ideas relating to God's existence. However, ideas of God in an individual could also arise spontaneously, from nature or from any other source at any time in their life. This is said to demonstrate that ideas for the existence of God have occurred in many forms throughout human history.

As far as is known, there was no knowledge of God's existence before humanity's existence. This fact raises an important question – is God a human "invention" or did God "find" humans? Because these things can't be proven, this leads to the reliance on belief, or mystery, for answers.

In the twentieth century, the traditional religious and social ways became less clear-cut. The world shrank – international travel was more available and, towards the end of the century, the internet brought every possible religion and type of spirituality (and much else) into everybody's home. And then it all even became accessible on their mobile phones. People became ever more able to select which religious or spiritual path they wanted to follow – or to choose multiple paths or no path at all.

Reduction

The net outcome of this has been a significant reduction in the number of people attending formal religious services. However, this does not necessarily mean that there has been any reduction in the belief in something "more" – it perhaps merely means that people have become more willing to exchange the certainty of belief that formal religion offers, for the mystery of spirituality.

During the twentieth century there occurred a significant migration of people – for two main reasons. Firstly, people began to migrate and seek asylum in relatively safer countries in order to avoid oppressive regimes. And secondly, people migrated in order to seek better economic opportunities. These two reasons are not necessarily mutually exclusive, and in both of these instances people often migrated with their religions and customs intact.

This huge movement of people caused dramatic changes to the religious and social structure of many countries. For instance, over a relatively short period of a few decades, the United Kingdom changed from a wholly Protestant Christian country to a multicultural one. Now there are almost as many people participating in non-Christian religious services – for example in mosques, synagogues, Sikh gurdwara, or Hindu temples, than there are attending Christian services.

Most people and their social and religious traditions, coexist relatively happily alongside each other in towns and cities in many countries. However, as with any sort of change (social or otherwise), there have been pockets of unrest and discord both within the host populations and between the host and new groups. Sometimes this discord can take generations to diminish.

The purpose of this long concluding description has been that, borne out by the statistics given above, there appears to be no real reduction in the vast majority of people who believe in the existence of God or at least hoping for something else, for something "other". What seems to be changing however, is that fewer people are attending formal religious services, and individuals, families, and whole societies, are evolving as different cultures merge and mix.

Good or not so good

It is now imperative to look back at personal

experience. Most people believe in God in some form or other, as statistics have shown. What makes these people so sure? Are the majority of eight billion people right or wrong? And what makes them accept belief over fact?

In most peoples' lives, mysterious and unexplainable things seem to occur. Some of these "happenings" may be seen as good, even wonderful, some not so, and to others they might even seem terrible. But in most of these cases, they are described as "God's will." Because people can find no earthly reason for these events, they turn to the idea that God, or a their "guardian angel," "guiding spirit," or something similar, has intervened in their lives.

Evidence that can be factually proven has to be believed whether it is liked, or not, but evidence without a factual basis is subject to individual opinion and interpretation.

With regard to belief in "God" in whatever shape or form God takes, ideas can be drawn from scriptures and other such writings, from the comprehensive contents and workings of nature (including the human mind and body), from unexplained events or happenings in an individual's life, and from other sources. These ideas and opinions become the basis onto which a person builds his or her life. These ideas may not be factually correct, but they are treated as fact by the individuals concerned.

Therefore, to answer our original question – Does God exist? – the answer for most people is an emphatic yes! This belief is the rock, however precarious it may seem to others, onto which people can and do build and maintain their lives.

It is true that personal experience can be more valuable than facts. This experience, this form of knowledge can, as previously noted, fill the void of life's meaninglessness, of the bleakness that some people experience.

So yes, God, in various shapes and forms across the world and in different cultures, does exist for all those who want God to, for all those who choose to believe in something higher or greater. There seems to be an utterly compelling pull that attracts some people to believe and know that God – or at least something – watches over them, guides and protects them. They believe that everything will be alright in the end, so to speak. They believe that God is the reason for (their) existence. And existence, as we have seen, is the "root" of everything.

Chapter 4 Truths

- God exists for everyone who wants God to exist.
- The mystery of God still remains because there is no tangible proof that God exists.
- Belief in God does not need to include participation in an established religion or adherence to religious doctrine.

Jot down any thoughts you may have about "Does God Exist?":

Chapter 5

Knowing Love

In a similar manner to the previous chapter, there are few widely held and provable facts available about love, particularly the type of love that is found in a relationship between two people. For practically everyone, love is a wholly personal experience, that is, it happens in the mind of each individual and it can potentially affect every single person at some time in their lives.

It cannot be proved that someone has any particular type of experience at all. However, it would be clear that a person, through their actions, is experiencing a great many, for example, while driving a car or eating a meal. It is probable that multitudes of people have exactly the same experience of any particular thing or activity, but it can never be fully known or proved by anyone else.

Obvious to say, each person can only know for certain what is going on in their own mind at any one time. This is the reason why it has to be agreed that each person's experiences are unique. Not one person's thought can be completely shared or known. Not even someone who is very close to a person can know what is "going on" in their mind.

Every woman and man, whether they like it or not, has to live life on their own. This might be the principal single cause of mental distress in life, but more of this later.

The purpose of life …

In order to understand the basis for love to exist, we need now to ask some related questions.

The first question is, "What is the purpose of life itself?" If the purpose is understood then we can continue. But some might say, "There is no purpose!" This may or may not be true, but within the limits of what is known most people (most of the time) nevertheless desire to continue living life.

The main and the most fundamental answer to this question of life's purpose is, simply put, to live a life and to live it to the full by using all the "tools" that are available to us. In most situations, life has to continue to happen while ensuring that it extends through producing offspring. Everything else is secondary. There is no choice in this, it is innate.

Every person (and all living beings) have to first accept that they are already living before any search for life's purpose can take place, or before finding out what life has to offer. Just in simply living, there is much to do; there is much to think about, to experience, to explore. Basic needs have to be continually met – such as eating, excreting, resting and keeping warm and dry. Achieving these things can take up much of life's time.

Even in extreme situations, for example, if someone chooses to end their life, then this is acted upon while the person is living – it is one of *life's* choices.

People have all sorts of ideas about life's purpose – ideas that range from the simple to extreme, from traditional to supernatural. And religious and spiritual ideas form a huge category of these ideas.

However, if we stick to the basics that underpin an

individual's life, there can be no escaping the fact the most fundamental purpose of life is to multiply – this occurs so that life, and our existence (as discussed in the first part), can continue to be lived.

… and its meaning

Once we have discovered life's most fundamental purpose, there is a divergent, yet closely allied, final question that. This question is, "What is the meaning of life?" Many people struggle throughout their lives to find an answer to this question – they may have a singular answer to this, or they may have multiple answers, or their ideas about this may be continually changing.

This question is more difficult to answer than the more clear-cut question of life's purpose. We can't be so sure about what meaning life has. This leaves each person to choose whatever meaning they please – whatever meaning is most acceptable to them.

But this is not necessarily an easy choice. In fact, because of this uncertainty, life's meaning is likely to be one the greatest causes of mental unrest, if not distress, that people have. In order to answer this question, a person has to go through a very difficult, possibly even traumatic, process in order to determine and establish a satisfactory answer. And once a person has found an answer to this question, they then have to verify it to themselves, once or continually, all on their own; the meaning of life is a very personal question.

It is not surprising, therefore, that one of the most popular answers to this question about meaning, lies in the belief in God. Meaning is often linked to the idea of God – and to the idea that God created individuals and perhaps created individuals on Earth in order to carry out God's particular wishes.

An individual might decide to seek meaning, or, they might choose to not think about it at all. In fact, many people choose the latter and choose to live material lives from day-to-day. They live quite satisfactory lives without thinking about life itself, or any alternatives. Some times in peoples lives – for example in adolescence – we are more likely to think about life's meaning than at other times. Teenagers sometimes have a very stressful time trying to find meaning – and trying to find good enough reasons to be alive. Sometimes they fail. Sometimes they give up. In other cases they don't bother, or accept quite quickly that the task is too difficult, or not worth the effort. Yet, most succeed

– and they succeed whether they end up becoming significant achievers on the one hand, or spending life muddling through as best they can.

Tools

In life, each person has a set of tools that enable their lives to function. These "tools" are limited to the tasks at hand and there are very few unused tools in the toolbox, so to speak. This toolbox is comprised of a body and a mind which include, for example, a heart to pump blood, a stomach to digest food, a brain to think, and so on.

And to ensure that life continues into the future, to ensure that we produce offspring, we have both physical and emotional tools available to us. On the physical level we have reproductive systems, and on the emotional level we have means that draw, and bind, two people together. An essential part of our "emotional toolkit" is called love. And this is not only available to humans; through biological observation we can see this happening in many life forms albeit via different ways and means.

physical need – in a similar way that animals (as far as we know) experience sex; it can take place as a physical act with what appears to be very little sensual feeling or emotion.

Types of love

As mentioned, there are different types of love, or different objects of affection. For example, the love of a child by a parent, the love of a sexual partner, the love for a mother or father, sister or brother. A similar emotion occurs when one simply loves life, or when one loves God, or a religious figure such as the Buddha, Jesus, Mohammad, or Vishnu. One might even feel love when we see particular landscapes, hear our favourite songs. We might "love" our football teams, or certain paintings, or our home. Each person has their own list and their own levels and strengths of feeling.

Love is different from liking. Liking has the opposites of hate, or anger; liking can be manipulated and created. Similarly, feelings such as desire, passion, longing, companionship, attachment, and yearning are not love – yet they can accompany love and be felt alongside it.

Love alone seems to be different; it has no opposite

and it doesn't necessarily happen when a person wants it to. Love seems to have its own agenda.

How love happens

So how might we gauge how this unique phenomenon happens? Primarily, we gauge how it happens for each person through observation, inquiry and discussion. At the beginning, when two people fall in love, there seems to be a glow surrounding them. During this stage, they often exhibit a type of new-found playfulness and a kind of secretive joy in the idea of spending time together. This type of love isn't something that can be engineered or arranged – but it is something that is more likely to occur in certain circumstances than others. Sexual intimacy accompanies this type of "being in love" feeling, but, as mentioned, sex can happen without this "in love" feeling, as can friendship.

Unlike laughter, or sex, love cannot be made to happen at any time or place. Love can catch people unawares, it is uncontrollable. There appears to be some yet-unknown alchemy or magnetic force that draws two people together. Sometimes the seeds of love exist between two people, but it takes some time for those seeds to flourish. At other times, it appears like an avalanche or tsunami of unexplainable feelings that burst within one, or both, of the participants all at once.

To create that meeting, so many things have to come together all at once, even going back in time through births, generations and locations. The chance for two people to meet at the same place at one particular moment in time and to make contact with each other and for love to happen, can be nothing less than astonishing and not possible to explain. Do these meetings happen purely by chance? Or are they in some way planned? Is there a reason why they happen? The answer to these questions, in part, depends upon the participant's beliefs and circumstances.

And once love has begun between two people, does it ever go away? Love certainly changes. It matures with age and familiarity. Love can either deepen or reduce with time; sometimes it is forgotten and only revived through memory. Sometimes positive feelings of love transform into something negative, and sometime this leads to break up. But whether love between two people ever ends entirely is subject to debate.

Those who have loved are certain of its existence. For those for whom it hasn't happened, they can only wonder at the possibility of it happening at any moment. As has been said, love is the only personal experience, out of the multitude that people have, over which there is little or no control. This is what makes love special.

Is love knowable? Those who have had the experience will give an emphatic "Yes." But we don't fully know how or why it occurs. Religious people might say that God causes it to happen – we can't know this. However, what we do know, is that the intense feelings that it can bring about are often the most central, and the most meaningful, part of people's lives – and that the reasons why it happens are shrouded in mystery and wonder.

Chapter 5 Truths

- Love cannot be manipulated; its source remains a mystery.
- Life's *purpose* is to live and multiply. Life's *meaning*, is up for the individual to decide.
- Sex is not love.

Jot down any thoughts you may have about
"Knowing Love":

Chapter 6

Fragility
and Uncertainty

Everything in life is going swimmingly and then, out of the blue, bang! Things change and life falls apart a little, or a lot, or massively. Things once thought to be solid and unbreakable are torn apart in a flash. What is going on?

Fragility and uncertainty exist in life from the start. They are there in the first moments in the womb, right through the ups and downs that happen in a person's life, to the end, and to death. Uncertainty never stops, not even for a second. The only certainty is that death will occur – but not how or when it will take place.

For religions people, there is the possibility of life after death. What that possibility might be is determined by the religion followed; none of the different religious ideas about life after death are completely universal.

Survival Instinct

Humans, and all life forms, appear to have an innate (built-in) capacity or instinct to survive regardless of the circumstances. For instance, a tree can survive in a crack on a barren rock or in a desert – and a person can survive a catastrophic car crash or a heart attack. This capacity to survive (the "survival instinct") has existed throughout history in all life forms. It has existed right from the beginning of life on Earth, if not before.

What would happen if there wasn't this drive to survive on a moment-to-moment basis? This drive to carry on living no matter what? Even in the worst-case scenarios – when circumstances are too catastrophic for life to continue – the survival instinct to carry on living still exists. Life hangs on until the very last moment before it is overcome.

In every moment, all life forms carry on living as if unaware of the future and the impending end of everything although there are notable exceptions – the most obvious being people. Despite this knowledge, individuals are not only able to continue living but most are capable of enjoying life's riches – happiness, beauty and contentedness – as well as enduring its reverse, its 'darknesses' – sadness, pain, and illness – as if life would continue forever.

Chapter 6 Truths

- Nothing is certain except death.
- Most life forms have a "built-in" survival instinct.
- For some people uncertainty can be reduced by choosing a religious belief.

Jot down any thoughts you may have about "Fragility and Uncertainty":

Chapter 7

Differences Between People

There is only one "thing" that all people, as well as everything else, have equally in common – and that is that all things exist. In an earlier chapter, we saw that there can be no degrees of existence; this means that no one person, no body, can have any more or any less existence than anyone or anything else. Every person, and all things, exists equally.

But apart from our equally shared existence, all things and all people have seemingly endless physical differences. Moreover, all sentient, conscious, beings have an endless amount of mental and emotional differences. This means that individuality and difference can be recognised in each other, and that difference is a fact of life. There are various degrees of difference between things and people – from subtle to extreme – but difference itself is universal.

Unless something is copied and multiplied by machines, most natural phenomena have differences that are easily noticeable. While not necessarily unique, a person's body, height, or eye colour will be different to another person's – and the whole of that person will be noticeably different. Every physical phenomenon can be "measured" and noted by others – which means that these differences can be proved.

Thoughts and emotions on the other hand, cannot be proven. The exact nature of these cannot be known. They are always unique to each person and cannot be directly experienced by anyone, or anything, else. The only way a person can communicate particular thoughts to others is through words, actions or sounds that are spoken, written or shown via physical expressions.

The strength of an individual's emotions can range from mild to forceful. Some emotions and thoughts are positive and to be welcomed, while others are seen as negative, "bad" and unwanted. The inner life of an individual – an individual's inner thoughts and "conversations" – occurs almost non-stop throughout every day and night except when in deep sleep or in a similar state.

Most of the time, and despite the fact that we appear to have more consciousness than other living beings, we humans do not have control of the content of our thoughts or our visions. However, some of us – for example various religious people such as monks or nuns – are able to develop more control of our thoughts, as well as our emotions, through practices such as meditation and prayer.

But for most people we have relatively little control. Sometimes, thoughts become destructive to ourselves and to others – to varying degrees. "Dark" thoughts range from relatively mild ones such as having a poor opinion of another person, to dwelling on that and carrying out undeserved negative criticism. This might then lead to actual disagreement with another person – and this disagreement might range from a minor disagreement to a huge argument or ultimately even to war. Our thoughts are all played-out in the world, between people; but they also occur within our own minds. The mind can be a "noisy" place indeed – and one might say that the noisier our own minds, the more our differences might play out as disagreements in the world.

Differences in thought can become disagreements between people when comparative judgements are made in a person's mind. The negative implications of this then often expand, and these comparisons (whether vocal or written) then occur between groups of various kinds, clans, organisations, and nations. Similarly, disagreements – whether due to different emotions or to different physical wants – also take place in and between other life forms, such as animals, birds and fish.

In human society, disagreement often occurs on the basis of all kinds of difference – such as between the rich and poor, the strong and weak, between genders, ages, between people with different skin colours, different levels of intelligence, and different physical and mental abilities. Disagreement can occur on the basis of different societal expectations, different cultural traditions, and different religious ideas. The world is full of difference and many of these differences have remained with us for centuries or longer; they have not changed significantly through time and possibly never will.

Equalities and Inequalities

Where there is difference, there is also often perceived inequality of some kind. It is in the mind that thoughts of inequality begin and where the problems start. People will never all be completely equal in all aspects – and perhaps we wouldn't want that because it would make everyone the same. Difference can be celebrated, but more often than not, it seems to cause huge upset.

Although it does occur, there is little call from people wanting less – less physical possessions, less money, or less power – than other people. It is very rare for a poor person to not want to be rich, but there are a great number of people who would like more equality with those more powerful or wealthy than themselves.

In recent times especially, there has been protest against, and social unrest because of, perceived inequalities – for example, the perception of the inequality of women compared to men. Perceived inequality has also perhaps increased since globalisation and since we have been migrating between nations more often. When societies and cultures meet and mix, then physical, as well as cultural, differences can cause people to feel unequal in various ways – for example in situations of racism or xenophobia. But inequality can also happen within cultural or racial communities – for example between people from different towns or between people with disabilities and those without.

Historically, wise thinkers have given us a way of coming to terms with inequality and a way of avoiding conflict over difference. It's been one message without much variation across the centuries – common to every language and every culture …

Kindness

The message is simply to be kind to one another. And, when we are kind, peace and more good things – such as happiness and joy – follow. When we are kind, the differences between us are not dwelled upon.

No matter the differences in their skin colour or nationality – the world's wisest people throughout history have all taught a very similar message; that is, that we should all treat our fellow human beings with equal mutual respect and tolerance and, "Do to others as you would have them do to you."

Some people choose, wilfully, to disregard kindness, and while they continue to do so, disagreements due to difference will prevail. But kindness is part of being human, and every person has the capacity to be kind to some degree.

Chapter 7 Truths

- Differences always exist.
- Kindness dispels differences.

Jot down any thoughts you may have about "Differences between People":

Chapter 8

Bodies

Section One: The Individual Person

The individual person is made up of a body and a mind that together form an excellent design. Every human has a body with which they can see, touch and feel themselves as well as the world around them. No one has yet created anything that is better designed than the bodies we already have. Nor has anyone created any body parts that are better designed. All designs have limitations – for example we cannot fly like birds and we don't have the sense of smell that dogs have – but our bodies, together with our brains, are perfectly designed for the purposes of being human.

Body parts can be transplanted into another body in order to replace damaged or worn-out parts, and the body can be cloned, but neither of these things improve the body. Robots, or mechanical parts are, at least as of yet, nowhere near as good as the original human body. The design of devices such as hearing aids or glasses serve specific and useful purposes, but they are not as good as the original design; they are not as good as having naturally excellent hearing or eyesight.

The human body is designed to live and grow throughout a lifetime. It is pre-programmed to change and develop continually from conception, through life, through death, and to disposal. The human body grows from nothing before the moment of conception, and nothing of it, after death and decay, is left at the end.

But this begs the question, who designed the egg and sperm in the first place? This question, along with other similar ones we have already met, doesn't have an answer. In this Pocket Handbook to LIFE, it has already been shown that human beings, and all beings, are limited. Every thing is limited in and to what can be done and what can be thought. There appears to be no item in the toolkit for living life that is not needed. No extra tool yet to find a current use for that we can know for certain. As human beings, just like every other being, we have to accept our limitations. On the plus side, we have every "tool" we need to live full and satisfactory life; to live any other type of life is alien to us and is the realm of science fiction.

When we say that the body, along with the mind, has been "designed", it implies that there was a designer. Did anything at all (for example planets or people) come to exist of their own accord? Or through evolution? Or were they created with an original intention by a "designer"? This is part of the great mystery talked about earlier in this book.

Existence and God

We concluded earlier that existence itself had to come before anything material was created – and that therefore existence itself was also likely to be the "designer" and the creator of everything that is in existence. Many people in various places in the world have called this entity "God", and over time, various religions have been created around the idea of God. Myths too, abound. Some religious people believe that God created them as individuals, and that God "watches" over them throughout their lives until they die.

Bodies

But this cannot be proven. What *can* be proven is that a male person's sperm has to come into contact with a female person's egg in order for a human body to be created. This mostly occurs through the act of having sex, but can also sometimes take place in a laboratory. This initial contact is called the process of "fertilisation", and it is out of this process that a *seed* is created. Seeds form the beginning of nearly all life forms on the planet. Like other life forms, the human "seed", the embryo, then begins to grow with nourishment – and out of this the adult human body, the mind, and consciousness, come about.

Consciousness

With regard to the latter, it is known that consciousness is lost if blood supply to the brain is interrupted – for example as occurs with a stroke. From this, we might deduce that consciousness initially commences after the blood in the embryo has been formed and has reached its developing brain. This happens in the human embryo around eight weeks after conception. So we know that without blood flowing through the brain there would be no consciousness – but beyond this, nothing concrete is known about it. We only know that consciousness can be aware of existence.

Sex repeated

As the body grows and puberty happens, the desire for sex arrives seemingly out of nowhere. Most human beings find themselves attracted to members of the opposite sex – and this desire is necessary for reproduction. The fact that this desire is a pleasurable experience is an essential part of the reproductive process. It helps to encourage a man and woman to engage in sex, as well as to stay together and to want to keep creating more children – thereby ensuring that the human species survives.

The first baby is born, and whatever the circumstances surrounding the child's conception and birth, it is usually experienced as something profound. The birth is a wonder for anyone who is present – and is often the most treasured experience of the parents' lives. The fact that a living being has been created feels like a miracle. For most new mothers, after all the pain of childbirth, seeing her child for the first time is a moment of joy and comes with a huge sense of achievement. This living being grew inside her, was fed by her, and she will now continue to feed and nurture it. For many women, this can be the most fulfilling experience of their lives.

But, bodies fail. Bodies always die. Babies die, children die, teenagers die, adults die. There is no escape. Every sort of body, even the planet itself on which we all live, will eventually die.

Even the new born baby soon cries out – for food, or warmth, or comfort. Sometimes the child cries out and despite all efforts to comfort him or her, it seems nothing will satisfy. In the worst of circumstances, it can seem that years pass like this.

Angst

The child turns into a teenager and young adult who can find no satisfaction or fulfilment in life. They remain self-obsessed and nothing outside of themselves seems to matter. Slowly and painfully, in an agony of tortuous decisions, that child grows up and has to face the life-changing questions of "Where shall I go?" "What shall I be?" "Where do I belong?" "Do I belong anywhere?" and (perhaps the most difficult to answer) "Who am I?"

Sometimes, young adults feel lost before anything has had the chance to start. They feel lost because the world – everywhere and everything – seems alien. Lost because they can find no comfort or warmth anywhere, they can become ever more frustrated and angry.

Yet, people continue to live, and happiness, even if in just small moments, is experienced – as are all the emotions of grief, sadness, joy and pleasure. People may continue to live for 100 years or more, and all experience various degrees of both positive and negative emotions – no matter who they are.

People deal with their thoughts and emotions in different ways; sometimes people get bogged-down by negativity and allow it to affect their lives in ways that are destructive, others manage to find joy and happiness even through very difficult circumstances. Sometimes people choose to ignore the bad things that happen in the world – they suppress negativity within themselves as well as the outside world because they find it too difficult to deal with. At other times, people are able to face the difficult challenges of the world with peaceful acceptance and understanding. Usually, in most people's lives, a mixture of these reactions occurs and they live through times of mayhem as well as through times of relative peace.

When people become parents, the sense of responsibility for another human being can feel overwhelming. This starts from the moment of birth, to when the child leaves home, and beyond. Questions such as "Is my child still breathing?" turn into "Will my child learn to read?", to "Will my child make friends," to "Will my child come home drunk?" "Will they make someone pregnant?" "Will they come home at all?" Being a parent can often lead to both joy as well as to heartache. The job of parenting goes through many changes, but for most people it never truly ends.

Repeating

And then the whole cycle starts again for a new generation; a child is born and is a source of both joy and pain for their parents – sleepless nights, joyful milestones, social worries, academic achievements, relationship difficulties, happy family occasions, academic failures, joyful graduations.

When the human being grows into middle age,

days and years often seem to pass by without notice. Youthfulness and physical fitness start to decline; hair turns gey and skin starts to wrinkle. Loneliness, or aloneness and separation, are often a feature of middle age as families grow up and move away, and childhood friends disperse. Even for those who have experienced strong family bonds, we are all individual beings, and this fact seems to come into stark focus as we approach old age. We come to realise that there has always been a distance, a space between ourselves and others, a solitary aloneness. And all of a sudden we are old.

Section Two: The Social Person

Through the use of our mind and our senses, we know our bodies pretty well. Advances in science have shown, in minute detail, what bodies consist of and how the various parts of our bodies function. However, although what happens physiologically is known, little is known about how a body becomes alive and maintains its ability to be a living thinking human being. Some people believe that God, or other metaphysical forces, may be the cause.

Medical sciences

Despite our intricate scientific knowledge of the physical body, very little is still known about the cause of many common physical ailments. The cause of many mental and emotional illnesses also remains a mystery to scientists. How can we know so much, and yet still have so much disease and suffering in the world?

As a whole, medical and technological advances, social growth, and better infrastructure, have meant that people are living longer lives than they did in the past. World population surveys have established that in about 1800, the average life expectancy globally was around 25 years. In 1850, the Office of National Statistics (ONS) was established in the United Kingdom and it found that this country's life expectancy then was about 40 years – a little more for women and a little less for men. In 2020, life expectancy had jumped to 79 years for men and 83 for women.

The causes of this increasing life expectancy have been widespread. Firstly, the introduction of clean drinking water and the building of sewage systems. Secondly, the ongoing advances in the medical sciences – particularly the introduction of new medicines and vaccines. In 1915, the most common cause of death in the western world was infection (of various kinds), now it is cancer and heart disease.

But advancements in medical science – in particular surgical and pharmaceutical developments – have caused new societal problems. These developments have meant that a large elderly population has been created worldwide, and, a large and growing number of this population have become too unfit to work. Some of these people have chronic long-term health conditions, while for others, their bodies have simply said, "I've had enough." Many then have little or no finances to pay for their upkeep.

Historical

Historically, the elderly were more likely to have been looked-after by their extended families in large, multi-generational family units. During the last 100 years or more, and particularly in the western world, families have tended to break apart with younger people moving away to find work and opportunity elsewhere. Family units have become smaller with couples having less children. It has become less feasible for the small family unit to physically and financially support two or more grandparents.

At the same time as the larger multi-generational homes have split into smaller units, they have also become scattered throughout the home nation, if not all over the world. All of these changes and the breaking of traditional ties leaves the older generation to fend for themselves or, in many instances, be moved into retirement or care homes.

Because modern medicine now exists across the entire globe (albeit at differing degrees of quality and accessibility), most people take advantage of these new ways of ensuring that their bodies and minds stay well, and of ensuring that they live the longest lives possible. That's the upside. The downside is that everyone knows life cannot go on forever and that, by living longer, life can get tougher.

What is known, is that living a longer life means that the frequency of contracting various illnesses and disabilities grows – and that many of these diseases and disabilities are not curable. Modern medicines can usually only help to treat the symptoms of ageing, rather than the underlying cause, and so the market for pharmaceutical medicines is surging.

Finance

According to WHO Global Heath Expenditure for 2018, the money spent annually by, or on behalf of, every person in the UK (including those in both public and private healthcare), was the sterling equivalent of $4,620. In the USA, this figure was $10,624, Germany $6,098, France $5,050, Australia $5,005, and Spain $3,576. These costs rise every year and at some point in the future a decision may need to be made as to whether these costs are worth it; are the results of these expenditures good value and worth having?

Social again

Since the start of the industrial revolution in the middle of the eighteenth century, and especially in the last 200 years across the world, there have been huge changes in the way that most people live their lives.

These changes include radical innovations that have taken place in practically every area of life including travel, entertainment, technology, communication, and in the home to name but a few. Huge changes have occurred in the way that we view and change our bodies – for example in the area of organ transplants or cosmetic surgery. And change has also occurred in our mental health and social relationships – divorce is more common, therapy or psychoanalysis has become the norm, and the internet now plays a huge role in the social lives of many people.

Life in the twentieth century is almost completely unrecognisable to that of the nineteenth century. This rapid change must be the greatest, by far, that has occurred in human history. Yet, it is interesting to note that while some religions have made certain adaptations in-line with these changes, there has not been a significant change in the way that God is viewed or thought-of. And globally, the majority of people still appear to believe in God's existence.

In conclusion, human beings are highly adaptable and we seem to take big changes in our stride. Perhaps there will be fewer changes in the next century. Or perhaps the changes will be even more dramatic; perhaps there will be even greater challenges to come, for instance, climate change. Or perhaps there are unseen and unknown challenges for humankind just around the corner, out of sight, ready to reveal themselves.

One thing is for certain; our history shows that human bodies are resilient and that we have an instinctive and resolute will to carry on through all kinds of challenges and changes. The future of humankind could be very good indeed, or it could become intolerable with, for instance, more war and disease. We will have to wait and see. The only other thing that we can know for certain, as individuals, is that for every body, and every thing, life will end and our bodies will decay.

While some spiritual or religious teachings say that life, in some form, continues into eternity. What we can know for sure, is that life happens in sequences, and that our bodies as we know them in this reality, will die and decay; life as we know and live it every day, ends for every body. That is certain.

Chapter 8 Truths

- Life is limited to a being's physical and mental capabilities.
- The possibility of experiencing happiness and beauty are available to all.
- Life will end.

Jot down any thoughts you may have about "Bodies":

Chapter 9

Right or Wrong

Every individual has the opportunity to make conscious choices throughout their lives – choices based on their knowledge, personal concerns, likes and dislikes, or political convictions. Directly or indirectly, these choices are between right and wrong; a right choice usually has good consequences for the individual, while a wrong choice often has bad consequences.

Sometimes a person can make a choice that affects others in a negative way, or is in some way unacceptable to them. Sometimes people deliberately make bad choices that they know are wrong – and are either willing, or not, to accept the consequences.

Sometimes, a person may only find out later whether a choice was the right one or not. Sometimes a choice that seems to be correct – based on the information available – turns out to be wrong. Usually, whether a choice is right or wrong is clear, but sometimes a grey area exists and there appears to be no clear difference between the two.

Choices are made by individuals prior to them committing to action. The individual must decide which course of action to take, or decide which way to respond to a request – either with a, "Yes, I will do it," or with a "No, I won't do it." We make large and small choices every day, before every single action that we take, and most of these choices are usually made within a split second.

Rules

But choices made by individuals are not made in complete isolation – they are made within a set of rules that help us make the right choices. Most individuals live in a social environment of some kind, be it a family, a group, a culture, or a nation, and these groups all have rules and customs (whether explicit or not) that members adhere to.

People adhere to these rules either consciously or unconsciously, willingly or unwillingly. Societal rules and norms are created, and develop, over time – not in order to serve the individual but to serve society as a whole. This means that the individual is only free to do what he or she wants within the confines of the society in which they live. Breaking the customs, rules, or laws of society results in social exclusion, censure, or punishment.

Most people abide by the rules governing them and live relatively peaceful lives. But many others fall foul of laws and customs and are isolated or censored as a result; these people are seen as needing to be punished in some way because they are either disrupting the peace, or because they are perceived as a threat in some way. The result of making "wrong" choices inevitably results in hardship for the individuals themselves, as well as (usually) for society at large.

In an earlier chapter, we looked at the universally accepted dictum of, "do unto others what you would have done to yourself." The feeling and expression of kindness, as advocated throughout history, has been shown to be an entirely free, naturally instinctive, and available-to-all, means of gently removing most individual and group ills. When we do this, we inevitably do what is "right".

Yet, despite this truth being known and accepted throughout the world, it hasn't been fully heard, adopted, or accepted by everyone – at least not all of the time as a practical reality in people's lives. It is the lack of this quality of kindness that has been frequently recorded as the reason why many individuals, and societies, are in the state they are in today. Negative occurrences such as dishonesty, argumentativeness, racism, sexism, violence, murder, and war – occur on small and large scales frequently. And every day our news reports of full of stories that have occurred as a result of these behaviours.

So why is this easy-to-understand and free-to-use quality – a quality that is part of our nature – not happen more often or on a more regular basis? One reason may be that being kind to one another might be seen to act against our individual best interests; sometimes, in order to make right choices, compromises need to be made. And further reasons to this universal question can be found in the teachings of great minds throughout history …

Afflictions

One of the most important of these teachings, is the teaching about the 5 human afflictions. These afflictions are inherent to human nature and affect us all. They can be described as the 5 most fundamental faults that each and every person has to confront and overcome, to varying degrees, in order to live good and happy lives.

The set of afflictions outlined here were formally given in the 2nd Century CE from much earlier teachings and other similar examples exist. They are the primary obstacles, one might even say, "poisons", that act against a good, happy and peaceful life within each person. They are: ignorance, identification, attachment, aversion, and fear.

The first of these, "ignorance", can be described as ignoring, misunderstanding, or not bothering to discover, the truth. Ignorance causes mistakes, blockages, and unnecessary diversions to occur in a person's life.

The second affliction is "identification." This can be seen as an over-emphasis on the self over others, and a self-importance (inflated ego) that creates false differences and comparisons with other people.

101

The third affliction is "attachment." Attachment refers to when a person becomes overly attached to things, possessions, or to other people. This type of reliance on things leads to an inability to let go of those things, and therefore to inevitable suffering for that individual. This inability to let go can "clog up" the smooth progress of a person's life.

The fourth affliction is "aversion", or strong dislike – of things, certain people, circumstances, places. Aversion causes negativity within the individual and therefore, ultimately, suffering. When a person spends their lives having strong aversions to things, then there is not room for the positive emotions of happiness, joy, or pleasure.

The fifth and final affliction is "fear." Fear is another negative emotion that can poison a person's life. Fear can take many forms – fear of certain people, of situations, of things, places, circumstances, poverty, loneliness, decay, or death – but the underlying sensation is the same. Love, as well as kindness, cannot simultaneously exist within a person at the same time as fear.

In fact, these teachings show that all of the afflictions can distract people from being kind to others, as well as from making the right decisions for themselves. And their existence within all of us seems to make it impossible, or at least very difficult, to bring an end to suffering and conflict in the world.

The afflictions form the basis of all the emotional "poisons" that afflict us – and within them are the myriad of negative habits and behaviours that we suffer from. For example, greed may arise from a person's *attachment* to things, or to their *fear* of not winning; self-importance may arise from their *aversion* of certain things or people or from their *identification* with something they feel gives them status – such as a relationship, house, or profession. The afflictions creep up on us through our ego's wants and desires – and without looking at the root cause of our negative traits, they can be very difficult to change or let go of.

But widely accepted knowledge of the five afflictions, or "poisons", shows that, if accepted and explored within each of us as well as in society as a whole, this could help to remedy most human ills. This kind of exploration has the potential to do away with conflict and crime – however large or small, local or international, whether racial, social, cultural or religious.

Kindness

All human beings naturally feel the emotion of kindness, at least at some point in their lives. To be kind is not new, it is an inherent part of the human psyche and of the human experience. If every person was kind to each other all of the time, as the ancient teachings summarise, there would be few, if any, problems between people.

As an example from 2021, Minneapolis, USA – if Derek Chauvin, the police officer who held down George Floyd until he choked to death, had shown compassion for George Floyd from the outset, the result would have been very different. With kindness, there would have been harmony between Chauvin and Floyd without death for one and prison for the other.

If, in 2022, the President of Russia, Vladimir Putin, had treated his problem over Ukraine with kindness instead of aggression and attack, he could have avoided the huge loss of life and devastation that occurred.

And in another example from 2023, this time between Israel and Palestine, enormous suffering has been caused, but with kindness from both, the result would be much different.

Being kind to every person (and every living being) has been shown many, many times to not only lead to peace and happiness for the recipients, but also to peace and happiness for those giving it.

There will still be human suffering such as from natural disasters and accidents. There will always be grief at the loss of a loved one, or physical pain from illness. And there will always be differences between individuals, families, races and nations. But when all of these sufferings are met with kindness as the main approach, and if all the people who find themselves in conflict are primarily kind to each other, then problems would be resolved far more successfully.

History teaches us (even when it teaches us what not to do) that when kindness affects our decisions, then peace will come as will greater happiness for all. No more anger in our homes, streets, towns and nations, no more domestic violence, gang violence, rioting, or war. By making the effort to be kind, we can all lead more peaceful and fulfilling lives.

People might say that a focus on kindness is too naïve, too unreal. They might say, "That's not how societies really operate." But consider this – if kindness is an integral part of being human, then it is also an integral part of our society. And despite what our endless news coverage of war and disaster tells us, kindness can in fact be seen everywhere in the world. It is seen in every country and culture across the globe; no matter how different we are from each other, kindness always exists.

Our bad news stories reflect that so many of us still make the wrong choice with regard to the five afflictions of ignorance, identification, attachment, aversion, fear. And not only does this happen in individuals, but our news shows that whole societies and cultures also suffer from these afflictions.

Wise thinkers and teachers from the whole spectrum of traditions, and throughout history, have taught that the world would be transformed beyond our imagining if each and every person was kinder to those around them. Our world would be a better place if we were to treat all human beings, beginning with ourselves, with compassion and kindness.

Chapter 9 Truths

- All choices that are made in the spirit of kindness are right choices because they are more likely to lead to harmony than those made without it.
- Kindness is an inherent human trait and exists in every one naturally.

Jot down any thoughts you may have about "Right or Wrong":

Afterword 1

Answering what Life and Living is all About

The natural order of things is evident everywhere in the world and when we look up into the night sky. It is evident in the shining of the sun, the movement of the stars, and the rising of the moon. The natural order defines how we live our lives every day. Scientists know that the shining of the sun is finite and that one day, billions of years in the future, the Universe and everything in it will cease to exist in its present form. But for now, while the sun continues to shine, the natural order continues; the Earth continues to spin around the sun and in turn, the seasons are created each year.

In the world's temperate zones, there are four seasons in each year. These seasons are always changing from one season to the next in the same order; spring always follows winter, autumn always follows summer. The seasons create the rhythm in which people live. Throughout time, when seasons change, people change with them, but the natural order that underlies everything remains as a constant in the background – always maintained and ongoing.

That is until more recently. Since the Industrial Revolution in the 18th Century, humankind has been altering this pattern and in recent years we have begun to see the effects of these changes on the natural order of things. One of these changes has been a change in the seasons with more unpredictable weather patterns happening all over the Earth.

This is frightening stuff, and sometimes deadly, and it means that the future for humanity is potentially bleak. Despite this, in its own way, nature "knows" more than humankind – and even if we destroy nature to the extent that we don't survive, it is likely to last a lot longer than us. Yet, in the very long-term billions of years into the future when the sun ceases to exist, then even nature as we know it on this planet will die.

But for now, if we want to survive alongside nature for as long as is possible, we humans need to remember how to live and look after ourselves in-line with what Nature will "allow." This is what living life to the full means and what this book is all about.

The Pocket Handbook to LIFE is about exploring the important things in life – life's fundamental building blocks – so that we can learn to build life on a solid footing rather than on insecure and shifting sands. It has been written in order to try to reveal the root truths of our existence – to get past the jumble of misunderstandings, miss-information, and social media opinions that exist in today's world – and get to the truth of what life is really about.

Once we become aware of, and really understand, these truths – both as individuals and collectively – then it could be the case that there is nothing more to do. It may then be that simply through our understanding, we will no longer want to hurt or maim our fellow human beings. At the very least, knowing these truths as a society, questioning them, discussing them, and continually testing and reviewing them, will help us to integrate them into our everyday behaviours. Doing so will allow us to create better lives.

Here is a summary of what we have explored in this book:

Existence Is Everywhere

Every body and every thing "has" existence. Existence is completely unique. It is an unequalled, constant and timeless quality. It is infinite and eternal because it cannot be brought into existence or destroyed. This is why some people call it God. Existence itself is unlimited, but every thing that has existence, is limited; everything that has existence ends at some point. There seems to be nothing unnecessary or missing in the make-up of any person or any "thing" that exists. Existence will never stop and there will never be anything else like it. Existence is life – it is all around us and it is everywhere.

The Universe and Cosmos

Existence existed before the Universe that we see

in the night sky existed; it existed before the stars, galaxies and our own solar system were even created.

The "place" in which our Universe exists has been called the Cosmos. The cosmos isn't necessarily just a "place" but can be seen as "space" itself – the space that is every where and extends throughout every thing. The Cosmos might therefore be seen as synonymous with existence – and therefore it can also be thought-of as God.

Multiples

It is easy to think of ourselves as individuals not related to anything else but nothing could be further from the truth. Every thing exists as "bundles" of multiple things all working together. It is only God, or existence itself, that can be thought of as having no equivalent.

Multiples are important – it seems that it is life's purpose not only to exist, but also to multiply – nothing more and nothing less. Various religions and traditions provide many, mostly similar, codes of practice around how and when we should multiply, but in the end, humans are free to establish and develop meaning for themselves.

Does God Exist?

Some say that there has to be something better, bigger, or just different, from the one life that we live and the world we see every day. The different world religions and cultures have many different variations of what that other world looks like, or how those other lives take place. But ultimately, they have all remained a mystery to us. Even adding current astronomic and scientific knowledge, people are still none the wiser about the existence of God; the mystery still remains.

The three main characteristics of God – all-powerful (omnipotent), all-knowing (omniscient), and everywhere at once (omnipresent) – are extremely difficult to accept as facts. The lack of facts is therefore replaced in almost everyone by a set of beliefs of some sort or another. Our beliefs are attempts to create a degree of certainty in an uncertain world.

As well as the three main characteristics of God, there is another important element which is that God is somehow directly personal but also totally transcendent; God helps each person and is able to "listen" to them, but can also do this for everyone and everything else at the same time. God acts as a personal spiritual "guide" who understands each individual's trials and tribulations, but is at the same time a transcendent "force" who is intimately responsible for each and every tiny, as well as immense, thing that happens in the Universe.

To date, religions have been geographically located – no one religion has been adopted fully, everywhere, and by all peoples. Beliefs in the 20th century increasingly draw from a variety of religious ideas and texts – from across the globe and from throughout history. If there is one God, people still have differing ideas about who, and what, God is.

Nevertheless, God or some-such exists for all those who want God to. In which ever culture, religion, nation, or form of any kind, God exists across the whole world. There seems to be an utterly compelling impulse in many or most human beings that impels them to believe and "know" that God guides and protects them. A belief in God helps people to feel that everything will be alright in the end. For many, it is a comfort to feel that God is the reason for their existence.

What are the different attitudes about God?

Atheist: the belief that there is no God and that the individual is all there is.

Humanist: a belief in the power of reason and science, and in the collective human potential and evolution, without any belief in God.

Spiritual: the belief in something more than the world we see without adherence to any of the world's major religions.

Religious: the belief in God as taught by one of the world's major religions.

Sometimes people may hold a belief in any combination of 2-4.

Knowing Love

In this book, before we looked at the topic of love, we explored the concepts of *purpose* and *meaning*. In chapter 3, we suggested that *purpose* can be most clearly seen in the fact that each person has to live a life and, if possible, multiply. Any other purpose is secondary.

The *meaning* of life however, is less clear. There

seems to be no one "given" reason at all. This means that every person is free to find their own meaning. This can be a daunting task and the cause of much mental distress for many people who feel that their lives lack meaning, or who have difficulty in finding meaning.

For others, they find meaning in love – whether that be for God, for the world, or for another human being. Love can be seen as the strong emotional "pull" that attracts and binds two individuals together. Love may happen to a person all of the time, or only at one moment, a couple of moments, many times, or sometimes never at all.

Love happens most obviously when two people experience deep love for each other – this type of love can be seen as one of the highest experiences that exist in life. Yet, each "lover" cannot know or experience the other's love exactly. Or if they do, they cannot prove it. Normally, this type of love is experienced between only two people rather collectively.

Love is different from liking. Liking has opposites in hate and anger. Liking can be manipulated and created. From all the emotions, the state of love alone seems to be different.

Love cannot be made to happen like laughter or sex. Love can catch people unawares; it is uncontrollable. There appears to be some as yet unknown alchemy that brings or draws two people together. Its occurrence might be experienced like an avalanche or a whirlwind. It might be like a tsunami of unexplainable feelings bursting forth within, or be a more gentle development of feelings that happen over time. Sex is not love but may increase the intensity of it. Liking is not love, but someone who is loved can also be liked, or not.

Does love ever end? It certainly changes; it matures with age and familiarity. Feelings such as desire, passion, wanting, companionship, attachment, and yearning, are not love, yet they are emotions that often happen alongside love.

A little of why love happens – why two people might fall in love with each other – might be understood, but nobody knows very much about *how* it occurs. Love can hold two people together or tear them apart. Love, and its intensity, remains shrouded in wonder and mystery. Religious or spiritual people might apportion its occurrence to God.

Fragility and Uncertainty

Everything in life is going swimmingly and then, out of the blue, bang! Things change and life falls apart – either a little, a lot, or massively. From the start of each human life there is uncertainty and fragility, and from then on, the uncertainty never ends, not even for a second. The only certainty is that death, the end, will happen – but we can't know when, how, or where. Every person has the choice to either accept this, or not. Every person can choose to live life as if it would never change or end, or choose to remember each day that it may end at any moment.

Both human and all life forms appear to have an innate capacity or instinct to survive. The origin of humanity's survival instinct did not suddenly start at a particular moment in history, instead, it has existed throughout history and throughout all life forms. Moreover, it has existed right from the beginning of life on Earth, if not before.

The survival instinct enables people to continue living. It enables them to enjoy life's riches – happiness, beauty and contentedness – as well as endure the reverse – life's darkness, sadness, pain, and illness.

Differences Between People

There are no degrees of existence, which means that every body, without exception, is equal.

But equality does not mean a lack of difference; each human being exists equally, but each human being is also different from all others – either physically, or mentally, or both intertwined. Our inner lives, our human thoughts, are also all different and unique. The one similarity is perhaps that continuous thoughts happen in all of us – but these thoughts can be positive – happy and good – or negative – bleak, hopeless, or bad. And despite our equality in terms of the reality of existence – in our minds, thoughts of equality and inequality arise.

But there is a way to reduce negative thoughts through techniques that control the mind and its racing thoughts. Another way in which, historically, negative thoughts were thought to be reduced, was through the natural instinct of kindness; many people from the worlds of religion, philosophy, and science, have repeatedly taught that being kind reduces or eliminates negative and harmful thoughts and actions. Yet, although kindness is an inherent and natural instinct, this natural instinct has been suppressed in many people.

Bodies

The body is limited to the life it is intended to live. Does this presuppose that the human body has a designer? The individual body is designed to reproduce so that human life can be sure of future survival. No matter how close a person is to another there is always a gap, which means that each person, as a body, is always alone.

Historical statistics clearly show that people's lives have grown much longer in length during the last 300 years due to clean water, sewage systems, and the introduction of infection control.

Nothing is ever certain except one thing – that each body, each living thing, will eventually die. Whether this death is complete – the complete end of the body's consciousness – or just another stage in an eternal flow of lives, depends on an individual's beliefs. But nothing is factually sure. Nothing is ever certain.

Right or wrong

Every individual has the opportunity to make conscious choices in life based on their knowledge, personal concerns, or convictions and intelligence.

These choices – directly or indirectly – can all be narrowed down to being between right and wrong. A right choice is usually "good" in that it is made out of kindness and positivity, and a wrong choice is usually "bad" in that it is made out of negativity and disregard for other people's physicality or emotions.

Human weakness can be summarised succinctly as the five basic afflictions that every person has to confront in their life. These afflictions can be thought of as obstacles or "poisons" that act against a good, happy and peaceful life for every person and for those around them. These afflictions are: ignorance, identification, attachment, aversion, and fear. The natural answer in all of life's situations and conditions is simply to be kind to oneself and to those around us.

Afterword 2

Truths: A Brief Summary

1st Truth: Existence is Everywhere

Without existence there can be no life. Existence is unlimited, whereas everything else is limited. God cannot come before or after existence. Therefore God, if God exists, is the same as existence.

2nd Truth: The Universe and Cosmos

There was existence before this Universe. The Cosmos is the natural order in which the Universe exists. And the Cosmos contains all of existence, all of everyone. So like existence, the Cosmos can also be compared to God.

3rd Truth: Multiples

The only single thing is existence, everything else exists in multiples. Life's purpose is to exist and multiply. There is no given meaning to life.

4th Truth: Does God exist?

God or some-such exists for those who want God to exist. Because there is no tangible proof that God exists, the mystery still remains. Belief in God does not need to include an established religion.

5th Truth: Knowing Love

Life's purpose is to live and multiply. Life, in itself, has no meaning. Sex is not love. Love cannot be manipulated. The source of love is shrouded in mystery.

6th Truth: Fragility and Uncertainty

Nothing is certain in life. All life forms have a strong instinct to survive. Only death is certain.

7th Truth: Differences between People

Thoughts create differences in people. Differences will always exist. Kindness removes animosity.

8th Truth: Bodies

Life is limited to a living being's physical and mental capabilities. Life will end, but the possibility of experiencing happiness and beauty are available to all.

9th Truth: Right or Wrong

All good choices tend to be right and all bad choices tend to be wrong. Kindness exists in everyone.

Epilogue

Throughout this Pocket Handbook to LIFE, the main aspects of life have been brought together to remind us all of what the basics of life are. In this age of diversion and distraction, we need this reminder more than ever. We live at a time in which the possibilities increasingly seem endless, but they often end up just being fantasy and fiction. When life is traumatic, or when it appears bleak and hopeless, instead of reminding ourselves of the amazing reality of the world in which we live, we distract ourselves with fantasies.

Our lives often seem limited – and in times of struggle, the limits of life seem to outweigh the possibilities and opportunities that exist for us in this world. The truth is that there is freedom to enjoy. We always have the opportunity to be more satisfied and content with life. The opportunity to be happy is always there however bleak our life may seem in any given moment.

The Pocket Handbook to LIFE is not a religious book, it is a book about life, yet the subject of God has appeared many times. This is because the subject, in a very broad sense, is of great importance to every person's life. It forms foundations and gives meaning. It is the rock that can, and does for many, stabilize and hold an individual together. It has the potential to bring the disparate parts of a person's life together to provide one clear meaning that helps a person to make sense of their life. Another way of looking at it, is that the idea of God in whatever form can prevent a person from falling off the edge into the darkness that too often seems to loom all around everyone in this fragile world.

Practically everybody knows love to varying degrees at least at some point in their lives. Love is probably the greatest emotion or feeling that one can experience. Each person can love themselves, their beingness, and/or anybody or anything else in the world and beyond. Many people love another person. Love might be the experience that provides the greatest sense of aliveness and worthiness in human beings. It enables us to say with conviction, "I am alive," "I am."

Life is all there is. There is no alternative to living and dying; it is how we think of it, how we choose to find meaning, and how we cope with it all, that matters.

THE END

Notes:

Notes:

Notes: